7 FAMILIES IN PUEBLO POTTERY traces the developments in style and technique in pottery making from generation to generation among seven Pueblo families. The pieces selected for exhibit represent a nearly complete chronological sequence of the potter's art within each family. The text of the catalogue traces the history of each family as far back in time as the oldest living member can recall, and provides statements made by each artist about his or her individual family work. Pottery making is an ancient art among the Pueblos and the fundamental process of pottery making has remained the same through time although style and design have changed as the exhibit documents. The examples of contemporary pottery on display give some measure of the diversity of current pueblo ceramics and will hopefully serve as an inspiration to young potters to continue their traditional art.

The collection of pottery on exhibit took two years to assemble. Contributions to the exhibit are from the artists themselves, private collections, and museums. The exhibit could not have been arranged without the generous and patient cooperation of each family. From the beginning, they were committed to the theme and the intent of the show. It is essentially theirs. Their comments in the text of the catalogue will perhaps enable us to see the development of the potter's craft through the eyes of the artists themselves.

"Pottery is a beauty and a precious thing for each home."

© 1974, Maxwell Museum of Anthropology, The University of New Mexico, Albuquerque, New Mexico.

2

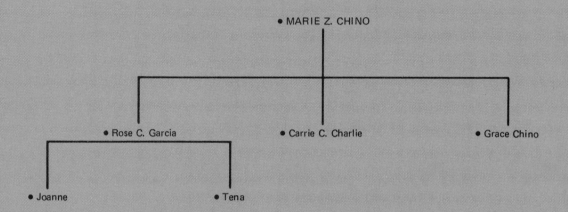

• MARIE Z. CHINO

• Rose C. Garcia   • Carrie C. Charlie   • Grace Chino

• Joanne   • Tena

• Represented in the show

CHINO
Acoma

Marie Z. Chino

"My mother, Marie Z. Chino, has been working in pottery for about 50 years and has handed it down to my sisters; Grace, Carrie and myself [Rose Chino Garcia]. She first taught us to grind pot sherds into temper to use in the clay mixture. The designs we use are mostly traditional Acoma designs. The deer with the heart line is from Zuni. The fine-line design we use a lot was revived by my aunt who found a sherd and gave it to my mother to use. My sister Grace and I have done some experimenting with combining designs, and we do a lot of the fine line. My mother has stayed with the old traditional designs.

3

Marie Z. Chino, Hohokam inspired design, canteen, black on white
1974, 5½ x 7 inches
Marie Z. Chino, Zuni deer with heart line, red and black on white
1974, 6 x 5 inches

Identification material with each photo shows the potter's signature, a description of the work, its date and physical dimensions (height x width).

Marie Z. Chino, black on white 1974,
5 x 6 inches

4

Marie Z. Chino, Mimbres fish design dish,
black on white, 1971, diameter 5½ inches

"First we mix our clay and add the temper of ground sherds. The forming of the pot is done by pinching if it is small or by coiling on the larger pieces. We use gourds for scraping and a pumice stone for sanding. The drying is done on the stove or in the sun for three or four days. The white slip is applied and polished with a smooth stone, then we paint them with the mixture our mother taught us how to make. We use cow and sheep manure for our firing and cover the pots with sherds so they don't get clouded."

Marie Z. Chino, black on white 1972, 6¾ x 9¾ inches

5

Rose Chino

6

Rose Chino, fineline black on white, 1972, 6¾ x 8 inches
Rose Chino, fineline black on white, 1974, 3½ x 3½ inches

Not pictured in catalog but present in exhibition

Joanne Chino, white indented designs, 1974
Tena Chino, black on white, 1974

Grace Chino

Grace Chino, black on white, 1974, 4½ x 5¼ inches
Grace Chino, black on white, 1974, 3¾ x 5 inches

Carrie Chino

8

C. Charlie, Zuni deer with heart line design, red and black on white, 1974, 5¾ x 6½ inches
Carrie Chino, Mimbres design canteen, black on white, 1974, 5½ x 4 inches

Lucy M. Lewis

"My mother, Lucy M. Lewis, began making pottery at about age seven and attracted public attention for her work in the 1950's. She is now seventy-seven years old. Our family would buy books to look up the old pottery designs and Dr. Kenneth Chapman from the Museum of New Mexico suggested to us to use the Mimbres designs and they have become very popular for us today. I [Dolores Lewis Garcia] was the first to use the Mimbres designs, then my sisters Emma and Mary began to use them. We have helped with publicity for other Acoma potters to bring more attention to the pottery of the Pueblo. My other sister, Anne Lewis Hansen, lives in California and works and exhibits with us during the summer."

9

Lucy M. Lewis, lightning design, black on white, 1971, 5¼ x 8 inches

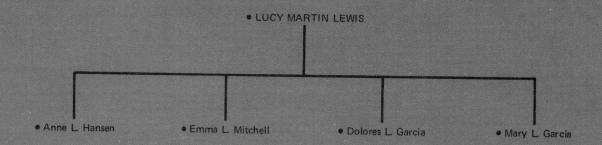

• LUCY MARTIN LEWIS

• Anne L. Hansen   • Emma L. Mitchell   • Dolores L. Garcia   • Mary L. Garcia

10

• Represented in the show

Lucy M. Lewis, tall jar, black on white, 1971, 8¼ x 8 inches

Lucy M. Lewis, black on white, 1972, 4 x 4½ inches

Lucy M. Lewis, red and black on white, 1971, 4½ x 6 inches
Lucy M. Lewis, black on white, 1972, 5 x 4 inches

Mary Lewis and Lucy M. Lewis, red and black on white, 1971, 3¼ x 6¼

Not pictured but present in exhibition

Lucy M. Lewis, Mimbres designed plates, 1971, diameters 3¼ inches, 3¾ inches

12

Lucy M. Lewis, red and black on white, deer with heart line design, 1968, 6¼ x 8½ inches

Mary Lewis Garcia

Mary Lewis, black on unslipped buff colored clay, Mimbres design, 1974, 3½ x 4 inches
Mary Lewis, black on white, 1974, 2¾ x 3 inches

"I enjoy making the pottery for others to enjoy. I'm glad I still have my mother to encourage me and show me how."

13

Dolores Lewis

14

Dolores Lewis, Hohokam design, black on white, 7 x 4¾ inches

Not pictured but included in exhibition:

Dolores Lewis, turtle, black on white, 1971, 1 x 2¾ inches
Dolores Lewis, saucer, Mimbres design, black on white, 1972, diameter 3¾ inches

Emma Lewis

*Emma Lewis, red and black on white, Mimbres design, 1974,
2½ x 2¾ inches
Emma Lewis, red and black on white, Zuni deer with heart line
design, 1971, 3 x 3½ inches
Emma Lewis, black on white, Mimbres design, 1974, 3½ x 3½
inches*

16

Anne Lewis Hansen

Anne Lewis, black on white, early 1970's, 2 x 2¾ inches
Anne Lewis, black on white, early 1970's, 3½ x 4 inches

NAMPEYO
Hopi

Nampeyo (unsigned), polychrome ca. 1907, 3 x 9½ inch diameter

Nampeyo

Nampeyo was born about 1860 at Hano, First Mesa, Arizona. She learned pottery making at a very young age and used the then popular Hopi designs. Although Nampeyo's technique in pottery was proficient before the Fewkes Expedition of 1895, the designs on prehistoric pottery found at Sikyatki by her husband Lesou, an archaeological crew member, inspired the great revival of Hopi pottery. Nampeyo and her husband consistently used these designs on their pottery, and today the style is carried on by their descendants. Nampeyo revived the low-shouldered shaped characteristic of the early Sikyatki wares. The design motifs, however, were not entirely from Sikyatki.

17

Nampeyo (unsigned), black on cream slip, early '20s, 17 x 18 inches

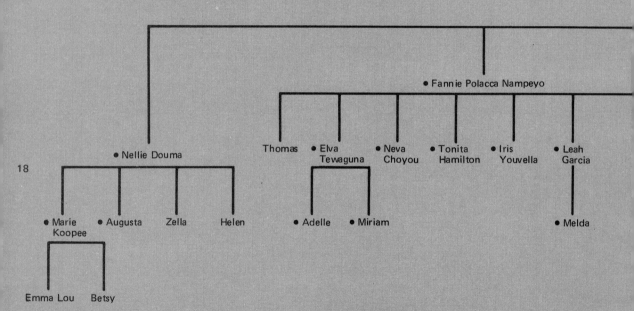

● NAMPEYO*

● Fannie Polacca Nampeyo

● Nellie Douma

Thomas ● Elva   ● Neva   ● Tonita   ● Iris   ● Leah
          Tewaguna   Choyou   Hamilton   Youvella   Garcia

18

● Marie   ● Augusta   Zella   Helen   ● Adelle   ● Miriam   ● Melda
  Koopee

Emma Lou   Betsy

● Represented in the show
* Deceased

LESOU*

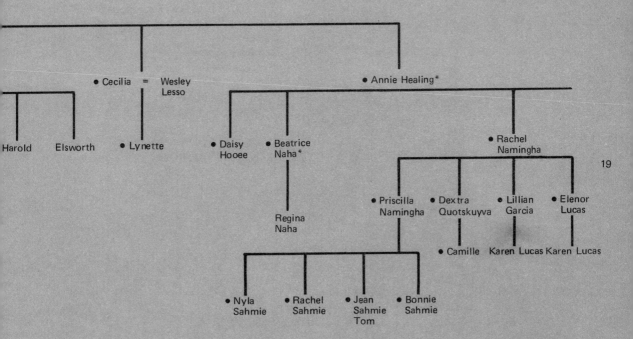

Harold   Elsworth   ● Cecilia = Wesley
                                      Lesso

● Lynette

● Daisy   ● Beatrice
  Hooee   Naha*

Regina
Naha

● Annie Healing*

● Rachel
  Namingha   19

● Priscilla   ● Dextra   ● Lillian   ● Elenor
  Namingha   Quotskuyva   Garcia   Lucas

● Camille   Karen Lucas Karen Lucas

● Nyla   ● Rachel   ● Jean   ● Bonnie
  Sahmie   Sahmie   Sahmie   Sahmie
                           Tom

Nampeyo (unsigned), polychrome, ca. 1930's?, 12½ x 8½ inches

Lesou visited other ruins, especially Awatovi, and designs from the ceramics of these ruins were also used. In the early 1900's the Fred Harvey Company at the Grand Canyon began promoting Nampeyo's work. When her sight began to fail, Lesou helped her with the painting. Her daughters, Fannie and Annie, also helped with the designing. During her last days she was cared for by her son, Wesley Lesso, and his wife, Cecelia. Nampeyo passed away in 1942. Annie Healing, the oldest daughter, and a potter in the Nampeyo tradition, passed away in 1968.

Lynette, Cecelia, & Wesley Lesso

C. Lesso, polychrome, 1973, 3 x 6¾ inches
Lynette Lesso, black on red, 1974, 2 x 3¼ inches

Cecelia Lesso

"I learned from Nampeyo, but I don't use
her complicated designs; I use many of my
own. Wesley helps in the preparation of the
clay and the gathering of the manure for
firing. Our daughter, Lynette, has taken up
pottery and plans to continue on with it."

Fannie Nampeyo

Fannie Polacca Nampeyo and
Leah Garcia Nampeyo

"We prefer to avoid the trader and deal with people personally. The trader says he'll make you famous and he gets richer and sells them for so much more. We make pottery for a living and we are glad that the designs have been taken over by the family. I (Fannie) was the first to take the designs from my mother and then hand them down to my family."

22

Fannie Nampeyo, polychrome, ca. early 1950's, 7¾ x 10¼ inches

Fannie Nampeyo, polychrome, ca. 1960, 3½ x 5¼ inches
Fannie Nampeyo, polychrome, ca. 1960, 4½ x 3¾ inches
Fannie Nampeyo, polychrome, ca. 1950, 3 x 4½ inches

Fannie Nampeyo, polychrome, 1972, 5½ x 7½ inches

Fannie Nampeyo, ashtrays, polychrome, ca. 1940's,
1¼ x 6½, 1¼ x 5½

Not pictured but in exhibition

Fannie Nampeyo, 1973, 2½ x 3 inches

26

Elva Nampeyo, polychrome, 1970, 5½ x 7½ inches

Not pictured but in exhibition

Elva Nampeyo, polychrome, 1973, 2¼ x 3 inches
Elva Nampeyo, plate, polychrome, 1970, 6½ inch diameter

Adelle & Miriam Nampeyo

Adelle Nampeyo, polychrome, 1974, 3 x 2½ inches
Miriam Nampeyo, polychrome, 1974, 2½ x 3½ inches

Leah Garcia Nampeyo

Leah Nampeyo, polychrome, 1972, 4¼ x 5¼ inches
Leah Nampeyo, polychrome, 1972, 5¼ x 5½ inches

28

Leah Nampeyo, polychrome, 1971, 3¾ x 7 inches

Melda Nampeyo

29

Melda Nampeyo, polychrome, 1973, 4¼ x 3½ inches
Melda Nampeyo, polychrome, 1973, 2½ x 2½ inches

Nellie Douma Nampeyo

"Nampeyo told me to teach my daughters how to make pottery and to keep the pottery making alive. Marie and Augusta have kept it up. I hope it never goes away. All the ladies do it. I use my pottery for a living and my son, Douglas makes dolls (kachinas). The whitish color to my pottery is from the way I fire it."

Nellie Nampeyo, polychrome, 1974, 6 x 7 inches

Nellie Nampeyo, polychrome, 1974, 1¼ x 6¼ inches

Marie Koopee Nampeyo

"I learned from my mother, Nellie, and Nampeyo. I worked with Nampeyo when I was small and used to bake the pottery with Nampeyo and Lesou. I use Nampeyo's designs and I work with my daughters to try to help them carry on the pottery making."

Augusta Nampeyo, polychrome, 1972, 2½ x 2½ inches
Marie Nampeyo, polychrome, 1973, 3¼ x 5¾ inches
Marie Nampeyo, polychrome, 1973, 2 x 4¼ inches

32

Annie Nampeyo

Annie Nampeyo, black on red, 1925,
2¾ x 3½ inches

Daisy Nampeyo, polychrome, 1974, 2¾ x 6 inches

Daisy Hooee Nampeyo

Daisy Hooee Nampeyo, polychrome, ca. 1950's, 3½ x 8½ inches

"The Ancient People didn't have pencils, so I learned to measure with my fingers. When I was small I would sneak a piece of clay and work where my grandmother could not see me. One day while my grandmother was sweeping, she found some of my small pieces hidden under the stove and she encouraged me to continue working. I married a Zuni man and moved there with him. I used to teach pottery making at Zuni High School. I go to Hopi to find the clay to use for traditional Nampeyo pottery, but I have also made Zuni pots from local materials. Too many children are not interested in the traditional work."

33

Beatrice Nampeyo, pre 1940

Beatrice Naha Nampeyo

She was briefly involved with pottery; but moved away after marrying. The date of her death is uncertain but is believed to be sometime in the 1940's.

34

Rachel Namingha Nampeyo

Rachel Nampeyo, polychrome, 1974, 4 x 7 inches

Rachel Nampeyo, polychrome, 1973, 3¼ x 5¼ inches
Rachel Nampeyo, polychrome, 1973, 3¾ x 6¾ inches
Rachel Nampeyo, polychrome, 1973, 3¼ x 6 inches

Dextra Quotsquyva Nampeyo

Dextra Quotsquyva, polychrome, wedding jar,
1974, 13 x 8 inches

"I started my pottery work around 1967 and have been working on it constantly ever since. My mother, Rachel, watched and supervised me. I would help my mother with the firing but began to fire on my own. I have experimented with the use of shells and turquoise on my pottery like some of the potters at San Ildefonso. My mother isn't happy about the break from tradition. I am always working on new experiments. I want to keep my pottery unique."

Dextra Quotsquyva, gray polychrome, 1974, 4½ x 8 inches

Dextra Quotsquyva, polychrome, 1974, 6 x 7½ inches

38

*Dextra Quotsquyva (Nampeyo), polychrome,
white slip, 1973, 10 inch diameter*

Priscilla Namingha Nampeyo

"I used to watch my mother, Rachel (Namingha), but I learned pretty much on my own. I put a lot of time into my fine line designs. My sister Dextra (Quotsquyva) and I are the only ones doing the real fine designs. I use my pottery for a living and would rather deal with the individual where I can get the price I want for my work."

Priscilla Namingha Nampeyo, polychrome, 1974, 7¾ x 8¾ inches

Priscilla Nampeyo, black and white on red, 1973, 10¼ x 9 inches

40

Priscilla Namingha Nampeyo, polychrome, 1973, 3½ x 6 inches

Lillain Gonzales Nampeyo
Rachel Sahmie Nampeyo
Jean Sahmie Nampeyo
Bonnie Sahmie Nampeyo
Elenor Lucas
Camille Quotsquyva
Nyla Sahmie Nampeyo

Bonnie Sahmie Nampeyo, black on cream slip, 1974, 2¼ x 2 inches
Camille Quotsquyva, black on cream slip, 1974, 1 x 2 inches
Rachel Sahmie Nampeyo, black on cream slip, 1973, 2½ x 3 inches
Jean S. Nampeyo, black on cream slip, 1973, 2½ x 3 inches
E. Lucas, black on cream slip, 1974, 1 x 3¼ inches
Nyla Sahmie Nampeyo, polychrome, 1974, 4 x 4½ inches
Lillian Gonzales, polychrome, 1974, 2 1/8 x 2¼ inches

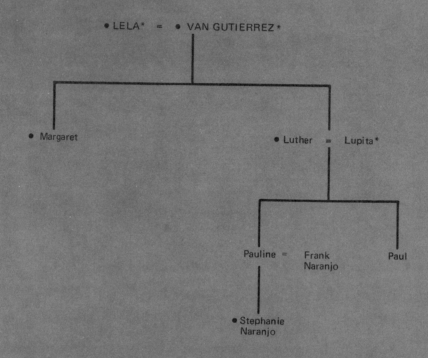

42

• LELA* = • VAN GUTIERREZ*

• Margaret

• Luther = Lupita*

Pauline = Frank
Naranjo

Paul

• Stephanie
Naranjo

• Represented in the show
* Deceased

Margaret and Luther Gutierrez

"Our pottery has come down to us through three generations. Our great-great grandfather, Ta-Key-Sane, was the one who created or started this kind of pottery, a long time ago. Most of the pottery he made was for his own use, like kitchen utensils that the ladies use nowadays, or for ceremonies. From what we can gather, through these years, our great-great grandfather was very artistic in making pottery and also in designing.

"Then my great grandfather took over the making and designing of the pottery. He also was very artistic, only he tried to improve it by adding more colors and making the pottery in more different sizes; big ones and small ones, also figures and animals.

"When my great grandfather passed away, my grandfather took over except this time my grandmother was making the pottery and my grandfather did the designing. During this time much more improvement was made because grandfather had been able to sell or trade to the white man for food and money. By this time my father, Van, was old enough to travel with my grandfather into the hills and mountains hunting game for food, but at the same time they would be hunting for clay of different colors; and also for flowers and roots for paints which would turn into differnt colors when fired. By the time my father was ten years of age, he was helping to design pottery, but he could also make pottery. He again made improvements mostly on designing and trying on different colors (slips). As for my mother, she did all the pottery making.

43

This is where we (my brother and I) came in. First my brother Luther: My father took him into the hills and mountains to show him where the different colors of clays could be found. Afterward he showed him how to mix them and the amount to be mixed. I remember how they used to sit day in and day out trying out different colors. If one color was not satisfactory to them they would add or take out some of the colored clay. As for myself by the time I was twelve years old, my mother had me making pottery; and by the time I finished high school, I could make pottery as good as my mother. She would say I am better because I have more ideas. Also my father showed me as he had my brother about the mixing of colors. Today I can make pottery whether large or small and I can also design. With all this knowledge that was handed down to us from generation to generation, today our pottery is the finest and most beautifully worked pottery in the world, and it is known the world over. Our pottery is all hand-made from the beginning; there is no commercial product used. This is all from Mother Nature.''

An approximate chronology for the Gutierrez Family is as follows:

Lela	Began 1890's
Lela and Van (started poly after married about 1905)	ca. 1900-1949 (Van's death 1956)
Lela and Luther	1949(50)-1966 (her death)
Margaret and Luther	mid 1960's-present

Lela, impressed bear paw design, black polished, ca. 1900, 7 x 5 inches

Lela and Van Gutierrez

Lela (painted by Van?), polychrome plate, ca. 1907, 2 x 11¾ inches

Lela and Van, polychrome with geometric design, ca. 1910, 6¼ x 6½ inches

Lela and Luther, Avanyu (water serpent) design wedding jar, polychrome, 1962, 12½ x 9½ inches

Margaret Gutierrez

Margaret and Luther, polychrome, 1974, 1½ x 2½ inches
Margaret and Luther, polychrome, 1974, 2 x 2 inches
Stephanie Naranjo, turtle, polychrome, 1974, ½ x 2¼ inches
Margaret and Luther, plate, polychrome, 1974, 1½ x ½ inches
Margaret and Luther, polychrome, 1974, 1 x 1 inches

47

Margaret and Luther, bear, polychrome, 1970, 1½ x 1¾ inches
Margaret and Luther, octopus, 1970, 1¾ x 2¾ inches

48

Margaret and Luther, polychrome, 1973,
4½ x 5¼ inches

Not pictured but in exhibit

Margaret and Luther, polychrome, 1974, 8½ x 6½ inches

Sarafina Tafoya

Unsigned, black polish, storage jar, bear paw impression, Ca. 1930, 23 x 19 inches

● SARAFINA* = GERONIM

● Margaret Tafoya   ●Camilio = ● Agapita Tafoya*

● Shirley   ● Mary Ester   ● Tonita   ● Lula   Lee = ● Betty   ● Virginia   ● Jennie   ● Mela
            Archuleta   Roller   Tapia   Ebelacker   Trammel   Youngblood

                                                                ● Richard

● William   ● Clifford   ● Tim   Phyllis   ● Melvin   ● Nancy   ● Nathan

50

● Grace   ● Joseph   Joe   ● Lucy
Medicine   Lonewolf   Tafoya =   Year Flower
Flower

                 Rosemary   ● Myra
                 Speckled Rock   Little Snow
                 (Apple Blossom)

● Represented in the show
* Deceased

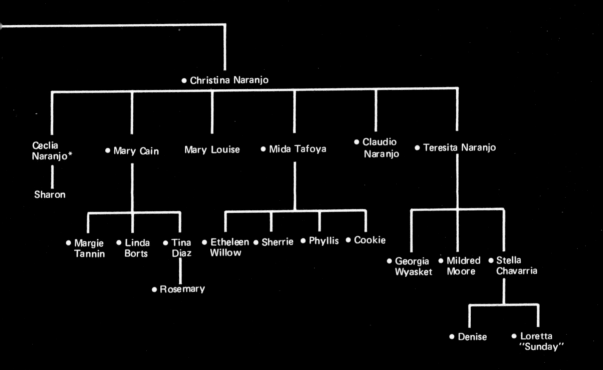

FOYA*

● Christina Naranjo

Ceclia Naranjo*   ● Mary Cain   Mary Louise   ● Mida Tafoya   ● Claudio Naranjo   ● Teresita Naranjo

Sharon

● Margie Tannin   ● Linda Borts   ● Tina Diaz   ● Etheleen Willow   ● Sherrie   ● Phyllis   ● Cookie

● Georgia Wyasket   ● Mildred Moore   ● Stella Chavarria

● Rosemary

● Denise   ● Loretta "Sunday"

51

Margaret Tafoya

Margaret Tafoya, red polished bear impression,
1973, 13½ x 15½ inches

"I started learning pottery from my mother Sarafina Tafoya when I was a child and I now use my pottery for a living. My mother would make the pottery while my father, Geronimo, would work in the fields. We didn't have big fields like the white man, just enough for the family. I would work with my mother until I could do everything myself. I am the only one to do the large storage jars like my mother's. I never had anyone to show them off; now my work is famous. "My mother taught me to do good polishing and that's the way I teach my girls. We really go over them to see if there are any small cracks or places where the slip has peeled off before we bake them. I start polishing the big ones in the morning and if I don't finish by noon I won't eat. You have to polish them all at once. Sometimes I don't finish until 3:00 or 4:00 in the afternoon.

"My daughter, Mary Ester Archuleta, married a San Juan man and does both kinds of pottery, the San Juan and the Santa Clara. We get our slip from the Santo Domingos for the black pottery.

"The bear paws are used on storage jars, water jars, and mixing bowls. It is a good luck symbol; the bear always knows where the water is. We use the kiva step, mountain, clear sky, and buffalo horn designs on our pottery. Sometimes we use the matte painted style."

Margaret Tafoya, black carved polished inside and out, 1974, 2 x 3¼ inches
Margaret Tafoya, black carved, 1974, 4½ x 5½ inches

Margaret Tafoya, red carved with buff paint, ca. 1950,
5¼ x 8¼ inches

53

Virginia Ebelacker

"I have continued to stay within the traditional designs and around 1951 I learned how to work in silver and turquoise and I use these materials on some of my new pieces. I used to help my mother, Margaret, with the polishing and I learned the pottery making by just getting involved in it. Since about 1968 I have been working on my own and I have taken many awards for my pottery. My son, Richard, has learned by being raised around pottery and stays with making miniatures."

*Virginia (Snowflakes) Ebelacker, black carved with
turquoise and silver setting, 1974, 11 inch diameter plate*

*Virginia Ebelacker, black carved with turqoise and
silver, 1974, 1½ ht—diameter 7½ inches
Richard Ebelacker, black polish, 1974, 3 x 4 inches*

Shirley Tafoya

Shirley Tafoya, black carved, 1974, 6½ x 7½ inches

Mary Ester Archuleta

Mary E. Archuleta, red incised polished (San Juan Style), 1974, 6½ x 6½ inches

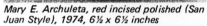

57

Mary E. Archuleta, red carved serpent design, 1974, 4 x 7¼ inches

Jennie Trammel

*Jennie Trammel, black polished inside and out
— carved, 1974, 3¾ x 5 inches*

59

Lula Tapia

Lula Tapia, black carved water serpent design,
1968, 9 x 9 inches

Tonita Roller
William, Tim, Clifford Roller

60

Clifford Roller, black polish, 1974, 2 x 4¼ inches
Toni Roller, black polish, 1974, 7 x 8¼ inches
Tim Roller, alligator, 1974, length 6½, height ¾ inches
Tim Roller, anteater (unsigned), 1974, 1¼ x 2½ inches
William Roller, black polish, 1974, 2 x 3 inches

The traditional black carved pottery is completely hand-made, uses only materials from nature, and is fired outdoors. Some designs on the pottery are:

"Serpent—The water serpent design represents various signs of nature; such as, lightning, clouds, waves, waterways, leaning trees, and mountains. The kiva steps add more significant religious meaning to the complete design.

Bear Paw—This design is the paw and claw prints of the bear. The bear and the path it takes are held in sacred respect by our Indian people.

Nature signs—The various significant signs of nature along with the meaningful kiva steps.

Feather—This design signifies the use of feathers in religious ceremonies and dress showing respect to birds.

Thunderbird—The design symbolically represents the forces of nature traveling through the sky in the winds.

Symbols of lightning, rain clouds, and rainbows may be included to depict strong wind carrying storms."

*Mela Youngblood, black polish with bear paw
impression, 1974, 15 x 10 inches*

Mela Youngblood

"I learned pottery making from my mother,
Margaret Tafoya, and have been seriously
working since 1969, after settling back at
Santa Clara after being in Holland. I have
been potting all my life on and off. I don't
like to do the same thing all the time; I like
to have a variety of shapes in pottery. I take
a very long time on my pottery because I
have set a high standard of perfection for
myself. My daughter, Nancy, stays at Santa
Clara (we have a home in Albuquerque also)
and works with my sister, Shirley "Berda"
Tafoya. Nancy has stayed with making
mostly miniature pots and my son, Nathan,
makes only peace pipes."

61

Nathan and Nancy Youngblood

Nathan Youngblood, peace pipe, 1974, 16½ inches long
Nancy Youngblood, miniature wedding jar black polish sgraffito,
1974, 2½ x 1½ inches

62

Melvin Ray Tafoya, black polished, 1974, 2 x 3¼ inches
Betty Tafoya, black carved, 1973, 3½ x 4 inches

Lee and Betty Tafoya

"We work together on our pottery, Lee does the forming and the carving and I do the finishing and polishing. Lee grew up in a pottery making atmosphere (his mother is Margaret Tafoya) but didn't start making his own until just the last few years. It was completely new to me when I picked it up. I think I am the only white woman working with Indian pottery, but the other chores of keeping the house keep me from making pottery full time. It is a very leisurely thing for me to do."

63

Christina Naranjo

Christina Naranjo and Mary Cain

"We work on our pottery together and have stayed with the traditional designs. The carving possibly started with a stick. There are carved pots in the ruins near White Rock. We use the carved Avanyu, or water serpent, as well as the geometric designs. I (Christina Naranjo) really began to make an effort on the pottery making after I was married."

64

Christina N., black polished water jar, ca. 1960, 13 x 14 inches

Christina Naranjo, black polished water jar with bear impression, 1974, 7 x 7 inches

Mary Cain

65

*Mary Cain, black carved Avanyu design, 1973,
4¾ x 7½ inches*

Christina Naranjo & Mary Cain, black carved Avanyu design, 1974, 5 x 8 inches

Mary Cain, red carved Avanyu, 1974, 6¼ x 6 inches
Tina Diaz, black-on-black, 1974, 2 x 2½ inches
Linda Borts, black carved, 1974, 1 x 1 inches
Rosemary Diaz, black polished oven pot, 1974, 1½ x 1½ inches
Margie Tannin, red-on-red, 1974, 1½ x 2 inches

Mida Tafoya

"My four daughters and I share the work on making the pottery; sifting the clay, soaking it, and adding the sand. I usually do the firing myself. I have stayed with the traditional designs and don't do much experimenting. I learned with my mother, Christina Naranjo, and used to work with my sisters. I enjoy doing my work very much. It gives me something to do for the day instead of an office job. It's a very creative job. I use it for a living."

Mida Tafoya, black carved wedding jar, Avanyu design, 1974,
7¾ x 5¾ inches
Mida Tafoya, black carved Avanyu design, 1974, 4¼ x 6½ inches

Etheleen Willow
Phyllis Tafoya
Shirley Tafoya
Cookie Tafoya

(Shirley), animal figure (unsigned), 1974, 2¾ x 4 inches
Etheleen Willow, black carved, 1973, 3½ x 5 inches
(Cookie), animal figure (unsigned), 1974, 2 x 2¼ inches
Phyllis Tafoya, animal figure, 1974, 5 x 2½ inches

Teresita Naranjo

"Pottery is handed down from generation to generation. As a little girl I used to watch my grandmother [Sarafina Tafoya] and I thought someday I was going to be put in the Potter's Hands, which is God. I dedicated myself and my precious hands to the Lord to do this pottery. I ask the Lord to help me as I grow older to help me show my talent to the world as an individual. I have taken my potteries to different places for exhibits and I have won many prizes and sweepstakes. From 1957 my pottery has become well known all over the world and since that time I know the Lord has done something wonderful for me and it was His Will for me to have this talent. It is not a hobby; it is my living. And I have been doing this all by myself; I have no one to help me, only God. And today I thank Him. He is the Potter. He molds my life and I mold the potteries. He has given me this talent to show my potteries all over the world and to show, exhibit, and demonstrate my potteries. God is always

69

Teresita Naranjo, plate black-on-black, ca. 1950's?,
2¼ x 12 inches diameter
Teresita Naranjo, red carved, 1974, 4½ x 2½ inches

70

Georgia Wyasket, black carved, 1974, 1 x 2 inches
Claudio Naranjo, black carved, 1974, 2½ x 2 inches
Mildred Moore, bear impression, black, 1974, 2 x 1¾ inches

with me. As I mold the potteries, I always think of God and how He molds my life.

"Claudio, my brother, is a deaf mute and when he doesn't have a job he makes potteries for a living. No one teaches him, it is his own will and he makes wonderful potteries.

"My daughters like to make potteries and they can do something for themselves someday. It is something special to them. If they don't have a job they can always make potteries. They don't want to forget their pottery making.

"Pottery is a beauty and a precious thing for each home."

Denise Chavarria, black carved, 1974, 2 x 8 inches
Stella Chavarria, black carved, 1974, 3½ x 4½ inches
Sunday Chavarria, black carved, 1974, 1½ x 2¼ inches

Stella Chavarria

"I am real proud of my mother. When I first
started I would watch her until I could do it
all myself. When I started polishing by
myself she would make me do it over and
over again until it was right. She has been my
major influence. I have been doing the
carved style since I began around 1970. My
daughters, Loretta "Sunday" and Denise,
have picked it up from me and do most of
their work after school."

71

72

Agapita Tafoya

Agapita Tafoya, black carved, ca. mid 1940's, 7 x 6½ inches
Agapita Tafoya, red carved, ca. mid 1940's, 3¼ x 6 inches

Camilio Tafoya

Camilio Sunflower Tafoya, black carved, ca. early 60's
4 x 8 inches

Camilio Sunflower Tafoya, red sgraffito, 1974,
4 x 3¾ inches

Grace Medicine Flower

Grace Medicine Flower and Camilio Tafoya

"Camilio is one of the first men potters to become known in the pueblo. He used to work with his late wife, Agapita, and did the traditional carved pieces. He is famous for his large carved pots and his sculptural horses. He now works with Joseph and does the sgraffito-style carving on miniatures.

"I [Grace Medicine Flower] worked with my father and really got involved seriously with the pottery around 1964. My first pieces were carved and I also did animal figures. Some of the first pieces are signed Grace Hoover (my married name). The later carved pieces done in the mid-60's were signed Grace , and the most recent pieces are signed Grace Medicine Flower . In 1968 we [Joseph Lonewolf and Camilio Tafoya] began to do the black and red style. My pieces today are mostly the red style. In late 1968 Camilio and I worked on the pottery together and we signed them together. In 1972 Camilio went to work at Joseph's house and continues to work there today."

Camilio Sunflower Tafoya, red sgraffito, 1974, 4 x 3¾ inches
Grace ⋈ & Camilio Tafoya, two tone black style and red
sgraffito, 1968, 3 x 4½ inches
Grace Medicine Flower ⋈, red sgraffito, 1973, 2 x 2¼ inches
Grace Medicine Flower ⋈ and Camilio Tafoya, red sgraffito,
1972, 2¾ x 3¾ inches

76

Grace Medicine Flower, black carved, 1966,
3¼ x 4 inches

Lucy Year Flower Tafoya
and Myra Little Snow

"I [Lucy Year Flower Tafoya] am from
Pojaque and am the only one making pottery.
I wanted to bring pottery making back, there
is originally one potter from there. I started
in 1959 with small rabbits, bears, and other
animal figures. In 1972, I began to work on
my low relief carving style that has become
my own. I have also done the traditional
carved and plain polished styles. My
daughter, Myra, picked up pottery making
from Camilio Tafoya who has been a major
influence on her. I am now experimenting
with new pottery shapes."

*Lucy Year Flower, black polish with bear paw & bear
impressed design, 1974, 5¼ x 4½ inches
Little Snow, black polish, 1974, 1¾ x 1¾ inches*

Joseph Lonewolf, sgraffito carving, polished black, 1969, 4 x 5 inches

Joseph Lonewolf and Rosemary
Speckled Rock (Apple Blossom)

Joseph Lonewolf is most noted for his intricate miniatures which are now using more than one slip for coloring. His designs are influenced by the Mimbres people whom he feels are his prehistoric ancestors. His miniatures range from 3/8 inches to about two inches and are much more difficult to complete than the larger pieces because of the exacting work. His daughter, Rosemary, has learned his methods and works in a similar style.

Rosemary Speckled Rock (Apple Blossom)

GONZALES
San Ildefonso

Rose Gonzales

Rose, black carved Avanyu black on black, 1971, 3½ x 8½ inches

Rose Gonzales, Tse Pe & Dora

"My mother, Rose Gonzales, is credited with being the first potter at San Ildefonso to do the carved-style pottery. She began her pottery making around 1929. She has done many demonstrations at various places and has taught many people her carving techniques. Her pottery is characterized by rounded edges on her carved areas and fine polishing. My wife, Dora, began working in pottery around 1969 and was influenced by her mother, Candelaria Gachupin, at Zia Pueblo where she was born. Dora began working in the traditional San Ildefonso matte-black-on-black style.

"I learned much from my mother and really began to work on my own in 1972. I began experimenting with the two-tone style that Mr. Popovi Da invented. Then I began to do the incised carving and setting turquoise stones. My wife and I work together and we're always working on new experiments. We're striving to hold on to tradition, but still experiment with new ideas. We have been teaching our four daughters; Irene, Jennifer, Candace, and Gail, and hope they will continue to make pottery. We have taken on my Indian name Tse-Pe (Eagle-Cane) as our professional and legal name. The designs we use most of the time are the Avanyu [thanksgiving for rain and water] and the bear."

79

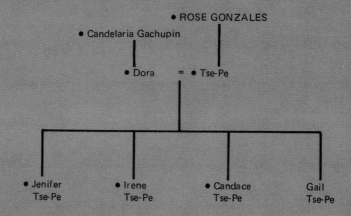

• ROSE GONZALES

• Candelaria Gachupin

• Dora = • Tse-Pe

• Jenifer
Tse-Pe

• Irene
Tse-Pe

• Candace
Tse-Pe

Gail
Tse-Pe

80

• Represented in the show

Rose, red carved Avanyu, ca. 1945, 5½ x 8¼ inches

Rose, black carved, ca. 1968, 5½ x 6½ inches

Candelaria Gachupin

Candelaria Gachupin, Zia bird design, polychrome, 1972, 9½ x 11½ inches

Tse-Pe and Dora

*Rose and Tse-Pe, two tone red and black carved,
1974, 4 x 6 inches*

83

*Dora, black on black, feather design, 1969, 5 x 4¼ inches
Irene, black sgraffito thunderbird, 1974, 3 x 5 inches
Candi and Jeni, black polish, 1974, 1½ x 2¾ inches*

84

Tse-Pe and Dora, black and red sgraffito with turquoise inset, 1974, 5¼ x 7¾ inches

MARTINEZ
San Ildefonso

Maria Martinez: polychrome water jar, made with her aunt Nicolasa Peña and is the piece Maria learned to make pottery on. It is signed and documented by Maria Martinez. The signature is in pen and also has a large "M" written on the bottom. *1909. Dimensions 10 x 12 inches*

Maria Montoya Martinez

Maria and her husband Julian Martinez were active potters in the traditional polychrome style of San Ildefonso before the famous matte black-on-black style was worked out by Julian in about 1919. They continued to work in the polychrome style until about 1926. The black-on-black style, which has made the Martinez family famous, has also helped to inspire more pottery making in the entire Rio Grande Pueblo area. The black-on-black style was so successful that polychrome was little used until the revival by Popovi Da in 1956 or 57. Maria and Julian were encouraged to sign their pieces by a trader early in their career. An approximate chronology of the signatures is as follows:

Marie   mid to late teens—1934
Marie and Julian   1934-1943 (his death)
Marie and Santana   1943-1956
Maria and Popovi   1956-1971
(Popovi Da helped her in the late 40's and early 50's but did not paint for her until 1956)
Maria Poveka   Undecorated wares only
                                   (none prior to 1956)

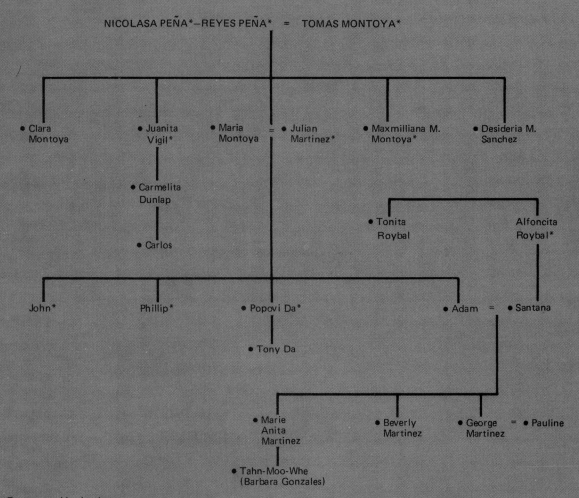

NICOLASA PEÑA*—REYES PEÑA* = TOMAS MONTOYA*

- Clara Montoya
- Juanita Vigil*
- Maria Montoya = • Julian Martinez*
- Maxmilliana M. Montoya*
- Desideria M. Sanchez

- Carmelita Dunlap

- Carlos

- Tonita Roybal
Alfoncita Roybal*

John*
Phillip*
- Popovi Da*
- Adam = • Santana

- Tony Da

- Marie Anita Martinez
- Beverly Martinez
- George Martinez = • Pauline

- Tahn-Moo-Whe (Barbara Gonzales)

86

- Represented in the show
* Deceased

Maria Martinez

Maria Povèka, black polish, ca. 1960,
10 x 10 inches

Marie "Century of Progess 9/28/34 For
HGH," black-on-black, 3½ x 6 inches

Maria, who at 90 is a living legend in Pueblo pottery, taught her family as well as her people the famous style of pottery making. Maria's four sisters; Maxmilliana, Desideria, Juanita, and Clara all worked in pottery. Juanita and Maximilliana did much of their pottery work as a team, one doing the shaping of the pot and the other decorating it. They did most of their work in the 1920's and 1930's. Maximilliana stopped producing long before her death in the mid 1960's. Juanita had several children and this kept her from working with pottery full time. Desideria worked mainly in the black-on-black style, also in the 1920's and 1930's, but was never as productive as Maria. Clara, the youngest sister, does most of the polishing of the pottery for the family and continues to help them today.

88

Marie/Santana, red on red, ca. 1948, 3¼ x 6¾ inches
Maria and Popovi, black feather design plate, black on black, 1960, 11¾ diameter
Maria Martinez, polychrome, 1919, 8¼ x 10½ inches

Marie/Julian, black on black, ca. 1940, 10 x 11 inches

Maria and Adam, black on black, 5¼ x 6½ inches

Marie and Julian, red polished, ca. 1940, 3 x 11½ inches

Marie, polychrome prayer bowl, ca. 1920, 3½ x 6 inches

90

Marie and Julian, polychrome, ca. 1935, 4 x 9 inches

Desideria Montoya Sanchez

Desideria, black-on-black, ca. 1930, 4½ x 6½

92

Desideria, black-on-black, feather design, ca. 1930,
7 x 8½ inches

Desideria, black-on-black, ca. 1930,
8½ x 7 inches

Maria Martinez and Clara Montoya

Clara (Martinez)/Maria, black polish inside and out, 3 x 6¾ inches
Signed by Maria in 1972

93

Maxmilliana Montoya

Anna, black matte on black, ca. mid 30's, 5 x 5 inches

94

(Maxmilliana Montoya) black polish, ca. 1930, 4 x 7½ inches

Juanita and Maxmilliana (signature in pen) Montoya,
polychrome water jar, 1919, 9¼ x 11¾ inches

Carmelita Dunlap

Carmelita Dunlap, black on black Avanyu design, 1969,
4½ x 7 inches
Carmelita Dunlap, black on black with feather design, 1969,
3½ x 5 inches

Carlos Dunlap

Carlos Dunlap, black on black, 1974,
4¾ x 5 inches

97

Carmelita and Carlos Dunlap

Carmelita Dunlap, red polish, 1974,
9½ x 9 inches

98

Carmelita Dunlap

"My mother Juanita passed away when I was young and I don't remember her too well. I watched Maria and Desideria making pottery and began around 1949 or 1950. I work with my son Carlos and we have stayed with the traditional ways of making pottery. Carlos began making pottery when he was about 12; he's now 16, and he will continue with it. We've experimented with the black and red style with the set turquoise but don't do it now. We feel better with the original way."

Tonita and Juan (Roybal)

Tonita & Juan, black-on-black vase, mid to late 1920's, 7 x 6 inches
Tonita & Juan, black-on-black, mid to late 1920's, 5 x 8 inches

Tonita, red and white-on-red, mid to late 1920's, 5 x 6¾ inches

99

Santana and Adam Martinez

Santana, candleholders, black style,
ca. 1945, 4¾ x 4 inches
Santana/Adam, black-on-black plate with
Avanyu design, 1973, 12½ diameter

100

"I started working with my Aunt, Tonita
Roybal, and when I married Adam I began to
learn from Maria. We work in a traditional
manner, but we have done the black and red
style. We will probably not do the set
turquoise stones. Adam helps with the
mixing of the clay and the gathering of the
firing materials, and he prepares the firing
grates. He also helps with the scraping and
sanding of the pottery. Clara
(Maria's youngest sister) does the polishing
for us and helps out with the other work
also. I do the painting after she has finished
polishing, and Adam will help fill in the
solid areas."

"You come back and take more pictures."

Marie and Santana, red-on-red plate with feather design, ca. 1948, 14½ diameter

Santana/Adam, black-on-black jar with feather design, 1973, 3¾ x 5 inches

Santana/Adam, black-on-black, 1973, 4¾ x 6¾ inches

Pauline, Beverly, and
Marie Anita Martinez

Pauline, black-on-black, 1973, 2 x 4 inches
Beverly, black-on-black feather design, 1973, 2¾ x 3½ inches
Marie Anita, black-on-black feather design, 1974, 3½ x 5½ inches

Tahn-moo-whe (Sunbeam)
Barbara Gonzales

"When I was a child I was influenced by
Maria and Santana, but I learned pottery
pretty much on my own. I was away during
school years but worked during the summers
on pottery. In 1972, I began working on the
black and red style and was influenced by
Popovi Da's and Tony Da's work. I try to
stay in a traditional framework with a
contemporary feeling. I originated the
hanging pots and windbells and I continue to
make them along with experimenting with
new forms."

103

104

*Tahn-Moo-Whe, two tone black with
sienna, sgraffito design, 1974, 2¾ x 4
inches
Tahn-Moo-Whe, two tone black with sienna
hanging pot with set turquoise stones, 1974,
3½ x 3½ inches*

*Tahn-Moo-Whe, black style with sgraffito
design with coral and mother of pearl, "The
Proud One," 1974, 7 x 6½ inches*

Maria and Popovi, polychrome plate with
feather design, ca. 1969, 14 inch diameter

Popovi Da

In 1956 or 1957 Popovi Da revived the
polychrome style that had been abandoned
at San Ildefonso; and Maria and Popovi Da
began to work in this style. Popovi Da also
tried to revive the old terra cotta and black
but he was unsuccessful in perfecting it
because the black paint used in the past
could not be found. He developed the plain
sienna finish and later the black and sienna
two-tone style.

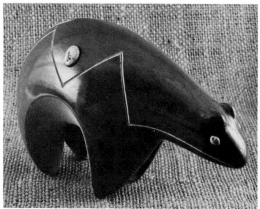

Da, red style bear with sgraffito design and set turquoise stones, 1970, 4 x 7 inches

Tony Da

"I began pottery making around 1966 when my Uncle Phillip passed away and I moved in with my grandmother, Maria Martinez, and my aunt, Clara Montoya. My father, Popovi Da, did experimenting with the two-tone sienna style in the early 1950's and finally came up with the perfected style in 1956 or 1957. My father didn't do much with the two-tone style on his work and he passed away in the fall of 1971.

"During the first two years my work was mostly black wares and about ninety percent of them used the two-tone style. During the second year, I began to set the turquoise stones. During the third year, I began to use lids on my pottery. I did the bears at the beginning, but no longer do them or the turtles. I am constantly working on more experimenting, and my latest work is involving a no polished surface but still using my incised carving (sgraffito). I am also doing some experimenting with cameo-type carving with different layers of slip.

"I incorporate the traditional with the contemporary with my own interpretation of the way I feel it should be done. I'd like to stay within the tradition, using traditional pottery making methods with contemporary techniques."

Da, two tone sienna and black with sgraffito carving, early 1972, 9½ x 8½ inches

Da, black style plate with sgraffito design in center, 1969, 2 x 11 diameter

Glossary

Terms are defined with specific reference to this exhibit.

Chaco Canyon (Classic Period): Chaco Canyon ruins are located in northwestern New Mexico. The designs on the pottery are characterized by the use of fine line and hatched areas. 1050-1200 A.D.

Small Chaco Canyon mug PIII, (b/w Classic Period), 1066-1192 AD

Hano: Tewa speaking village on First Mesa, Arizona. First Mesa is one of the three Hopi mesas located in northern Arizona. Original home of the Nampeyos.

Hano Polychrome variation, ca. 1896-?

Mimbres (Classic Period): Prehistoric culture in southwestern New Mexico and southeastern Arizona. Pottery from this culture, especially the Classic Period, is noted for its fine execution of design and the use of animal figures. 1150-1250 A.D.

Mimbres classic black-on-white bowl—1150-1250 AD

Polacca: Modern town at the foot of First Mesa, Arizona where the Nampeyo family now makes their home.

Polacca Polychrome Bowl—1800-1900 AD?

Sikyatki: A ruin in the old Tusayan (Hopi) province of Arizona. Many inhabitants moved from here to Awatovi (a ruin also in the Tusayan province) after Sikyatki was abandoned. The pottery from these ruins influenced Nampeyo designs.

Sikyatki Polychrome bowl—1375-1625 AD

Tewa: The northern Rio Grande Pueblos speaking the Tewa language.

Tularosa (Classic Period): Prehistoric pottery type from the southwestern portion of New Mexico. Designs are characterized by balanced solid and hatched areas. 1100-1300 A.D.

Tularosa Black/White Pitcher 1150-1300 AD—Pueblo III Classic Period

Black Style: Pottery made from any color of clay fired in an oxygen-reducing atmosphere.

Black Water Jar—Northern Tewa ca. 1910

Black-on-Black and Red-on-Red Styles: The use of a slip over a polished surface to create a matte (dull) design. The red or the black is determined by the firing.

Black-on-White: Black paint on white slip.

Carbon Paint: Paint made from a vegetable material such as the bee plant which carbonizes (blackens) with heat.

Coiling: A method of forming pottery by building up the walls with rope-like coils of clay.

Mineral Paint: Paint made from such minerals as hematite. The paint is usually mixed with a vegetable material to aid in the adherence to the surface of the pot.

Oxygen-reducing atmosphere: An atmosphere obtained in the firing of the pottery by smothering the fire with powdered manure to create a smoke whose carbon turns the pottery black.

Oxydizing atmosphere: An atmosphere obtained by a clean smokeless fire. An oxydizing atmosphere is necessary for the firing of the red pottery and the black-on-white pottery.

Polishing: A slip is applied to the surface of a dry pot and laboriously rubbed with a worn stone to bring about a smooth lustrous finish.

Polychrome: The use of three or more colors on a pot.

Red Style: Pottery made of a red clay fired in an oxydizing atmosphere.

Scraping and Sanding: Scraping is frequently done with a gourd to smooth over the coils used in the construction of the pot and to even out the walls. When the pot is dry, sanding is usually done with a pumice stone to prepare the surface for slip and final polishing.

Sgraffito: The scratching through the slip to expose the color of the clay beneath the slip. Among some contemporary Pueblo potters this effect is achieved after the firing.

Sherds: Broken pieces of pottery. The Acomas use sherds to grind into temper, but often designs are inspired from these fragments found in ruins.

Sienna Two-tone Style: Developed by Popovi Da. A technique where both the red or sienna and the reduced-black are on the same piece.

Slip: Clay which is thinned with water to a cream-like consistency to color the surface of a pot or to change the texture of the surface.

Temper: Any coarse material added to the clay to permit even drying and workability. Temper is also necessary to lessen temperature shock in the quick firing process. Common tempers are sand, ground sherds, and ground rock.

Terra cotta: Red earthenware clay.

Credits and Acknowledgments

Photography: Portraits, Rick Dillingham; Pottery and portraits (pp. 64, 65, 69, 79, 87, 93, 100), Dick Dunatchik; Annie Nampeyo pot (p. 32), courtesy Museum of Northern Arizona, Marc Gaede, photographer; gallery photographs of Nampeyo, courtesy Milwaukee Public Museum, Dr. Samuel Barrett, photographer, 1911; Photographic production, Martha Nufer.

Collection assembled and co-ordinated by: Rick Dillingham

Catalog: Beverly Barsook, Sally Black, Rick Dillingham, Steve Rhodes.

Exhibit Design: Dick Dunatchik, Bill Buck, Sally Black

Installation: Dick Dunatchik, Beverly Barsook, Sally Black, Bill Buck, Rick Dillingham, Martha Nufer, Carol Stout.

Lenders to the Exhibition: Mary Cain, Anita Da, Rick Dillingham, Carmelita Dunlap, Carlos Dunlap, Virginia Ebelacker, Anne Goodman, Barbara Gonzales, Maurine Grammer, Margaret Gutierrez, Beatrice Jones, Emma Lewis, Kathy Linn, Theresa Lonewolf, Adam and Santana Martinez, Maxwell Museum of Anthropology, Museum of New Mexico, Museum of Northern Arizona, Edna Norton, Dextra Quotsquyva, Tonita Roller, Juanita Roybal, Lucy Year Flower Tafoya, Tse-Pe and Dora and Mela Youngblood.

Special thanks to Christina Naranjo and Mary Cain for demonstrating pottery making methods at the opening reception.

A note of personal thanks is extended to all the potters represented in this exhibit for their patience and cooperation.

Acting Director, Maxwell Museum of Anthropology: Professor John M. Campbell.